Xmas 1986

WOMEN, HEROES,
and
a
Frog

NINA LEEN

all photographs by the author

Elaine —
My dear one;
Larry

W · W · NORTON & COMPANY
New York · London

W. W. Norton & Company, Inc., 500 Fifth Avenue, New York, N.Y. 10110
W. W. Norton & Company Ltd., 37 Great Russell Street, London WC1B 3NU

Layout by the author

Pictures previously taken for Life Magazine
reprinted here with the permission of Time, Inc.

ISBN 0 393 08624 0

Library of Congress Catalog Card No. 71-116125

Published simultaneously in Canada
by George J. McLeod Limited, Toronto

Printed in the United States of America

567890

We must laugh before we are happy for
fear of dying without laughing at all.

—Jean de La Bruyère (1645–1696)

Wrinkles should merely indicate
where smiles have been.

—Mark Twain (1835–1910)

What sunshine is to flowers, smiles are to humanity.
They are but trifles, but scattered along life's pathway
the good they do is inconceivable.

—Joseph Addison (1672–1719)

Happiness: A good bank account, a good cook and a good digestion.

—Jean Jacques Rousseau (1712–1778)

How happy the life unembarrassed by the care of business.
—Publilius Syrus, Maxim 725

It's a funny thing
that when a man hasn't
got anything on earth to
worry about, he goes off
and gets married.

—Robert Frost
(1874–1963)

By all means marry;
if you get a good wife, you'll become happy;
if you get a bad one, you'll become a philosopher.

—Socrates (c. 470–399 B.C.)

A man builds a fine house; and now he has
a master, and a task for life; he is to furnish,
watch, show it, and keep it in repair the
rest of his life.

—Ralph Waldo Emerson (1803–1882)

How it is I know not; but there is
no place like a bed for confidential
disclosures between friends. Man
and wife, they say, there open the
bottom of their souls to each
other; and some old couples
often lie and chat over old times
till nearly morning.

—Herman Melville (1819–1891)

Men always want to be a woman's first love; women have a more subtle
instinct: what they like is to be a man's last romance.

—Oscar Wilde (1854–1900)

Love—
   a grave mental disease.
      —Plato (427?–347 B.C.)

Not to go to the theatre is like making one's
toilet without a mirror.
                    —Arthur Schopenhauer (1788–1860)

History is philosophy teaching by examples.

—Dionysius of Halicarnassus
(died c. 7 B.C.)

You say there is nothing to write about. Then write to me that there is nothing to write about.

—Pliny the Younger (62–113)

If a man should importune me to give a reason
why I loved him, I find it could no otherwise be
expressed. . . . Because it was he, because it was I.

—Michel Eyquem de Montaigne (1533–1592)

Husband and wife come to look alike at last.
—Oliver Wendell Holmes (1809–1894)   .

There's only one pretty child in the world,
and every mother has it.

—Chinese proverb

God could not be everywhere
and therefore he made mothers.
—Jewish proverb

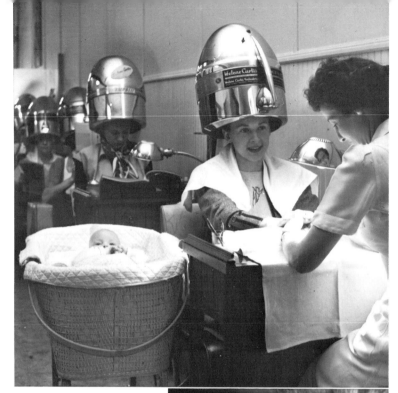

A mother who is really a mother
is never free.

—Honoré de Balzac (1799–1850)

If nature had arranged that husbands and wives
should have children alternatively,
there would never be more than three in the family
—Laurence Housman (1865–1959)

There is but one love, yet his shape is legion.
—François de La Rochefoucauld (1613–1680)

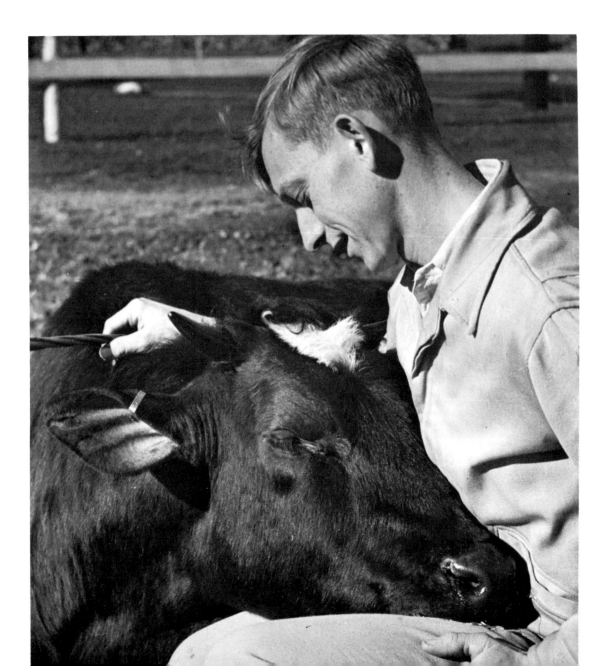

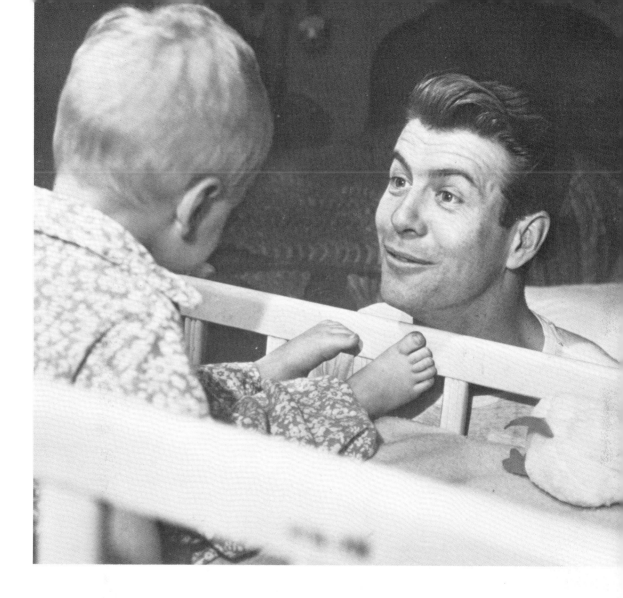

The word Papa gives a pretty form to the lips.
Papa, potatoes, poultry, prunes and prism are
all very good words for the lips.

— Charles Dickens (1812–1870)

There's a barrel-organ caroling
    across a golden street . . .
and the music's not immortal;
    but the world has made it sweet. . . .
        —Alfred Noyes (1880–1958)

Who hears music, feels
his solitude peopled at once.
—Robert Browning (1812–1889)

Light quirks of music, broken and uneven,
Make the soul dance upon a jig of Heaven.
—Alexander Pope (1688–1744)

He was a rationalist,
but he had to confess that
he liked the ringing of
church bells.
                    —Anton Chekhov
                        (1860–1904)

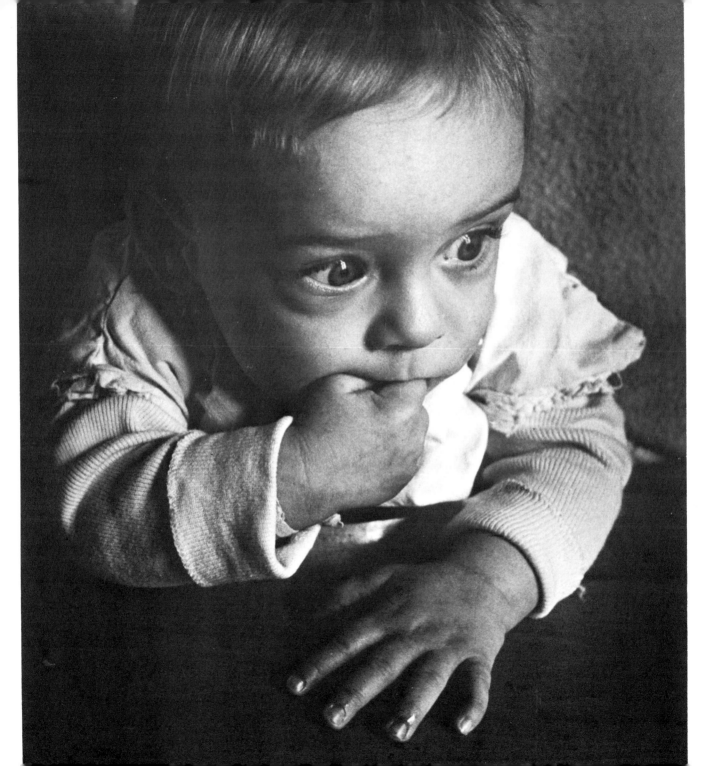

"There mustn't be any more war. It disturbs too many people." (1917) —An old French peasant woman to Aristide Briand

Suppose you go to war, you cannot
fight always; and when, after much
loss on both sides, and no gain on
either, you cease fighting, the
identical old questions as to terms
of intercourse are again upon you.
—Abraham Lincoln (1809–1865)

All history, so far as it is not
supported by contemporary
evidence, is romance. . . . That
certain kings reigned and
certain battles were fought
we can depend upon as true,
but all the coloring, all
the philosophy of history
is conjecture.

—Samuel Johnson
(1709–1784)

" . . . born with the gift of laughter and a sense that the world is mad."

—Rafael Sabatini (1875–1950)

No man is a hero to his valet.
                    —Madame Anne Marie Cornuel (1614–1694)

Most sorts of diversion in men, children
and other animals, are in imitation of fighting.
—Jonathan Swift (1667–1745)

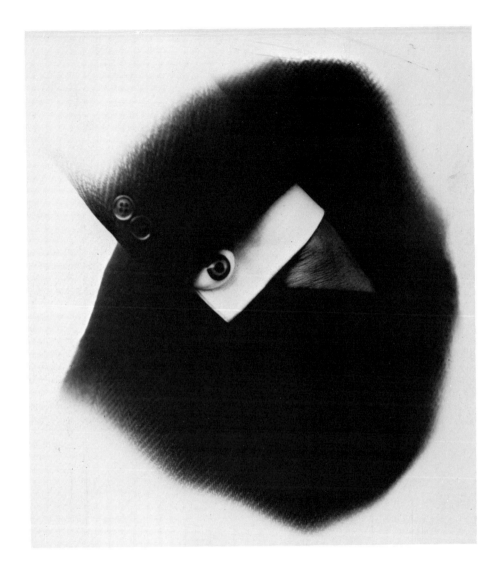

Yet he was jealous, though he did not show it,
For jealousy dislikes the world to know it.
—George Gordon, Lord Byron (1788–1824)

Flirtation, attention without intention.
—Max O'Rell (1848–1903)

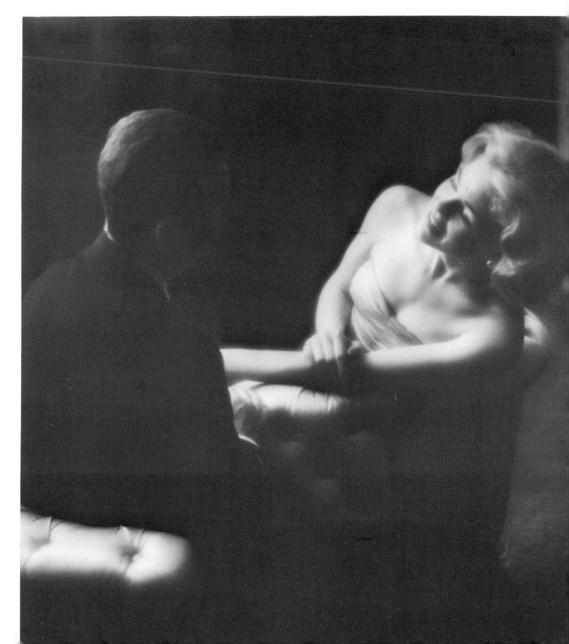

No one ever keeps
a secret so well
as a child.
—Victor Hugo
(1802–1885)

Ignorant people think it's the noise which fighting
cats make that is so aggravating, but it ain't so;
it's the sickening grammar they use.

—Mark Twain (1835–1910)

No one is happy all his life long.
　　　—Euripides (480?–406 B.C.)

Thank God for sleep!
And when you cannot sleep,
still thank Him that
you live to lie awake.
—John Oxenham
(1861–1941)

Sleep . . . peace of the soul,
who puttest care to flight.
—Ovid (43 B.C.–A.D. 17?)

Night brings our troubles to the light rather than banishes them.
—Marcus Annaeus Seneca (54 B.C.?–A.D. 39)

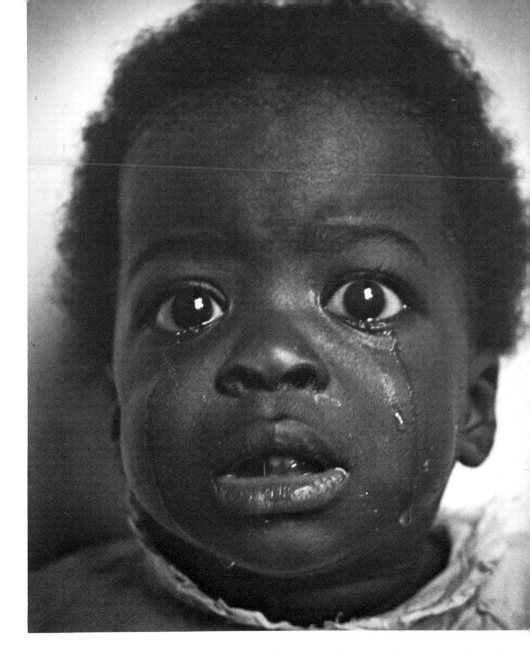

Tears are the silent language of grief.
—Voltaire (1694–1778)

A child thinks 20 shillings and 20 years can scarce ever be spent.
—Benjamin Franklin (1706–1790)

Associate with men
of good quality, if you
esteem your own reputation.
—George Washington
(1732–1799)
(written before 1748)

All actual heroes are essential men—and all men possible heroes.
—Elizabeth Barrett Browning (1806–1861)

Man is a cooking animal. The beasts have memory, judgment, and all the faculties and passions of our mind, in a certain degree; but no beast is a cook.

—James Boswell (1740–1795)

If Heaven made him—earth can find some use for him.
—Chinese proverb

Man is the only animal that can remain on friendly terms with the victims he intends to eat until he eats them.

—Samuel Butler (1835–1902)

The question is not,
Can they reason? nor,
Can they talk? but,
Can they suffer?
　　　　—Jeremy Bentham
　　　　　(1748–1832)

Just as a bird that flies about
And beats itself against the cage,
Finding at last no passage out,
It sits and sings, and so overcomes its rage.

—Abraham Cowley (1618–1667)

Even savage animals, if you keep them confined,
forget their natural courage.
—Cornelius Tacitus (c. 55–c. 17)

I like trees
because they seem
more resigned
to the way
they have to live
than other things do.
　　　　　—Willa Cather
　　　　　(1876–1947)

Take winter as you find him and he turns out to be a thoroughly honest fellow with no nonsense in him. And tolerating none in you which is a great comfort in the long run.

—James Russell Lowell
(1819–1891)

Work consists of whatever
a body is obliged to do, and
play consists of whatever
a body is not obliged to do.

—Mark Twain (1835–1910)

Even if a farmer intends to loaf, he gets up
in time to get an early start.

—Edgar Watson Howe (1853–1937)

All of the animals excepting man know that the
principal business of life is to enjoy it.
—Samuel Butler (1835–1902)

If you could once make up your mind never to undertake
more work . . . than you can carry on calmly, quietly, without
hurry or flurry . . . and if the instant you feel yourself
growing nervous and . . . out of breath, you would stop and take
breath, you would find this simple common-sense rule doing
for you what no prayers or tears could ever accomplish.

—Elizabeth Prentiss (1818–1878)

Leisure is the time
of doing something useful.
—Proverb

Oh! don't the days seem lank and long,
When all goes right and nothing goes wrong?
And isn't life extremely flat
With nothing whatever to grumble at?

—William Schwenck Gilbert (1836–1911)

Woman is at once
apple and serpent.
—Heinrich Heine
(1797–1856)

God created woman.
And boredom did indeed
cease from that moment,
but many other things
ceased as well. Woman was
God's second mistake.
—Friedrich Nietzsche
(1844–1900)

The desire of a man for a woman
is not directed at her
because she is a human being,
but because she is a woman.
That she is a human being is
of no concern to him.

—Immanuel Kant (1724–1804)

There are no ugly women; there are only women
who do not know how to look pretty.
—Jean de La Bruyère (1645–1696)

To a toad, what is beauty?
A female with two lovely pop-eyes,
a wide mouth, yellow belly and
green spotted back.
                    —Voltaire (1694–1778)

Grace is more beautiful
than beauty.
—Ralph Waldo Emerson
(1803–1882)

Sabina has a thousand charms
To captivate my heart,
Her lovely eyes art Cupid's arms,
And every look a dart;
But when the beauteous idiot speaks,
She cures me of my pain,
Her tongue the servile fetters breaks
And frees her slave again.
—From *Amphion Anglicus* (1700)

Habit makes everything, even love.
—Luc de Clapiers, Marquis de Vauvenargues
(1715–1747)

Art is man's nature; nature is God's art.
—Philip James Bailey (1816–1902)

"Use my eyes," said
a celebrated painter,
in reference to a model
that his interlocutor
thought frightful; "Use
my eyes, sir, and you
will find it sublime."

—Charles Gounod
(1818–1893)

The never idle workshop of nature!
—Matthew Arnold (1822–1888)

A weed is no more than a flower in disguise.
—James Russell Lowell (1819–1891)

Either do not attempt at all, or go through with it.
—Ovid (43 B.C.–A.D. 17?)

Where is human nature so weak as in the bookstore?

—Henry Ward Beecher (1813–1887)

And still they gaz'd, and still the wonder grew.
That one small head could carry all he knew.
—Oliver Goldsmith (1728–1774)

The extra calories needed for one hour
of intense mental effort would be
completely met by eating of one oyster
cracker or one half of a salted peanut.
—Francis G. Benedict (1870–1957)

We don't know one millionth of one per cent about anything.
—Thomas Alva Edison (1847–1931)

That there should absolutely be nothing at all is utterly impossible.
The mind, let it stretch its conceptions ever so far, can never
so much as bring itself to conceive of a state of perfect nothing.
                                                    —Jonathan Edwards (1703–1758)

Witchcraft, and all manner of spectre-work, and demonology, we have now named madness, and diseases of the nerves, seldom reflecting that still the new question comes upon us: What is madness, what are nerves?

—Thomas Carlyle (1795–1881)

What is mind? No matter.
What is matter? Never mind.
—Thomas Hewitt Key
(1799–1875)

O'er all there hung a shadow and a fear;
A sense of mystery the spirit daunted,
And said as plain as whisper in the ear,
The place is Haunted.

—Thomas Hood (1799–1845)

A house is never still
in darkness to those
who listen intently,
there is a whispering
in distant chambers. . .
Ghosts were created
when the first man
woke in the night.
—James M. Barrie
(1860–1937)

Courage is resistance
to fear, mastery of fear,
not absence of fear.
—Mark Twain
(1835–1910)

Who has seen the wind?
Neither you nor I;
But when the trees bow down their heads,
The wind is passing by.

—Christina Rossetti
(1830–1894)

It is wonderful that five thousand years
have now elapsed since the creation of the world,
and still it is undecided whether or not
there has ever been an instance of the spirit
of any person appearing after death. All
argument is against it, but all belief is for it.

—Samuel Johnson (1709–1784)

We spirits have just natures
we had for all the world,
when human creatures.
—John Dryden
(1631–1700)

Somewhere—in desolate wind-swept space
In Twilight-land—in No-man's-land—
Two hurrying Shapes met face to face,
And bade each other stand.

"And who are you?" cried one a-gape,
Shuddering in the gloaming light.
"I know not," said the second Shape,
"I only died last night."

—Thomas Bailey Aldrich
(1836–1907)

Good Americans when they die, go to Paris.
—Thomas Gold Appleton (1812–1884)

The passion of prying
into futurity makes a
striking part of the history
of human nature.
——Robert Burns (1759–1796)

Unintelligible answers to insoluble problems.
—Henry Brooks Adams (1838–1918)
(defining philosophy)

What sort of philosophers are we, who know absolutely
nothing about the origin and destiny of cats?
—Henry David Thoreau (1817–1862)

Women, cats and birds are creatures
that waste the most time on their toilets.
—Charles Nodier (1780–1844)

Love the sea? I dote upon it—from the beach.
—Douglas Jerrold (1803–1857)

The sea possesses a power over one's moods that has the effect of a will. The sea can hypnotize. Nature in general can do so.
—Henrik Ibsen (1828–1906)

Modesty died when clothes were born.
—Mark Twain (1835–1910)

All women's dresses are merely
variations on the eternal struggle
between the admitted desire to dress
and the unadmitted desire to undress.
　　　　　　—Lin Yutang (1895–　　)

Has a woman who knew that she was well dressed ever caught a cold?
—Friedrich Nietzsche (1844–1900)

Fashion is that by which
the fantastic becomes for
a moment universal.

—Oscar Wilde (1854–1900)

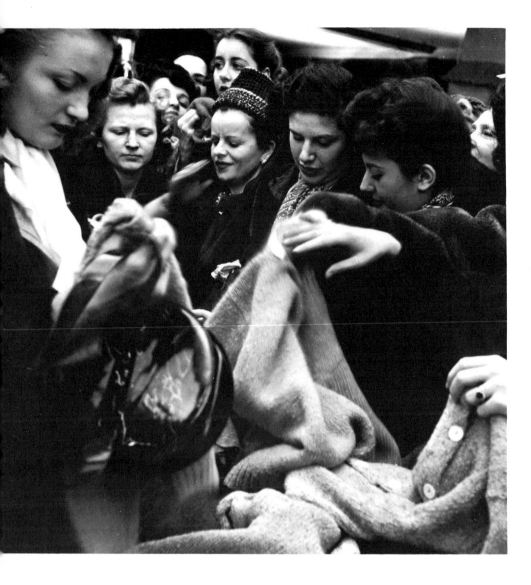

A woman is always buying something.

—Ovid (43 B.C.–A.D. 17?)

The whole trade
in the luxuries of life
is brought into
existence and supported
by the requirements
of women.

—Leo Tolstoy
(1828–1910)

Human felicity is produced not so much by great pieces of good fortune that seldom happen, as by little advantages that occur every day.

—Benjamin Franklin (1706–1790)

I have heard with admiring submission the experience of the lady who declared that the sense of being perfectly well-dressed gives a feeling of inward tranquility which religion is powerless to bestow.
—Ralph Waldo Emerson
(1803–1882)

When love and skill
work together
expect a masterpiece.
—John Ruskin
(1819–1900)

Employment is nature's physician, and is essential to human happiness.
—Galen (c. 130–c. 200)

You are not an author, as you are not an artist, unless
from your own heart you add to the treasures of art
something which would not have existed if you had not been born.

—Alphonse Karr (1808–1890)

A great city, a great solitude.
—Proverb

If children grew up according to early indications
we should have nothing but geniuses.

—Johann Wolfgang von Goethe (1749–1832)

The eyes of young men are curious and penetrating, their imaginations are of a roving nature, and their passion under no discipline or restraint.

—Joseph Addison (1672–1719)

Nothing will ever be attempted if all
possible objections must be first overcome.

—Samuel Johnson (1709–1784)

Life is a perilous voyage.
—Palladas (c. A.D. 400)

Old friends are best.
King James used to call for his old shoes;
they were easiest for his feet.

—John Selden (1584–1654)

There is a magic in the memory of schoolboy friendships;
it softens the heart, and even affects the nervous system
of those who have no heart.

—Benjamin Disraeli (1804–1881)

Gentlemen of the Jury:
The one, absolute, unselfish friend
that man can have in this selfish world,
the one that never deserts him, the one
that never proves ungrateful or treacherous,
is his dog.

—Senator George Graham Vest (1830–1940)

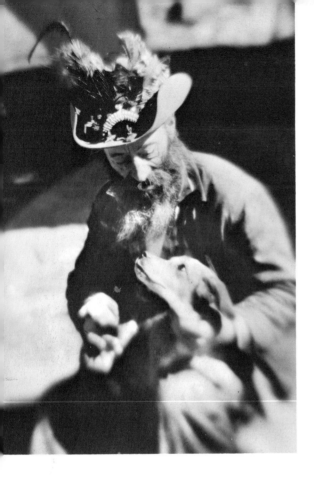

To his dog, every man is Napoleon;
hence the constant popularity of dogs.

   —Aldous Huxley (1894–1963)

Oh, the saddest of sights in a world of sin,
Is a little lost pup with his tail tucked in.
—Arthur Guiterman (1871–1943)

Great issues develop from small beginnings.

—Norman Vincent Peale (1889–   )

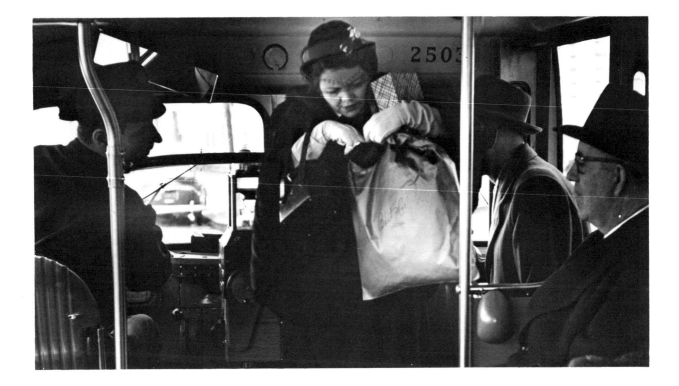

God grant us patience!
—William Shakespeare
(1564–1616)

There is nothing so bitter, that a patient mind
cannot find some solace for it.
—Marcus Annaeus Seneca (54 B.C.? A.D. 39)

The great hope of society
is individual character.
—William Ellery Channing
(1780–1842)

Nature, when she invented,
manufactured and patented
her authors, contrived to make
critics out of the chips
that were left!

—Oliver Wendell Holmes
(1809–1894)

There are no fools
so troublesome as
those who have wit.
—La Rochefoucauld
(1613–1680)

I found nonsense singularly refreshing. . . .
—Charles de Talleyrand-Perigord
(1754–1838)

Nothing is lost
on him who sees.
　　　—Thomas Moore
　　　　(1779–1852)

At twilight nature becomes
a wonderfully suggestive effect,
and is not without loveliness,
though perhaps its chief use is
to illustrate quotations from the poets.

—Oscar Wilde (1854–1900)